Eulogy on King Philip

Eulogy on King Philip
William Apes

MINT EDITIONS

Eulogy on King Philip was first published in 1836.

This edition published by Mint Editions 2021.

ISBN 9781513283388 | E-ISBN 9781513288406

Published by Mint Editions®

MINT
EDITIONS

minteditionbooks.com

Publishing Director: Jennifer Newens
Design & Production: Rachel Lopez Metzger
Project Manager: Micaela Clark
Typesetting: Westchester Publishing Services

Who shall stand in after years in this famous temple, and declare that Indians are not men! If men, then heirs to the same inheritance.

Address, &c.

I do not arise to spread before you the fame of a noted warrior, whose natural abilities shone like those of the great and mighty Philip of Greece, or of Alexander the Great, or like those of Washington,—whose virtues and patriotism are engraven on the hearts of my audience. Neither do I approve of war as being the best method of bowing the haughty tyrant, Man, and civilizing the world. No, far from me be such a thought. But it is to bring before you beings, made by the God of Nature, and in whose hearts and heads he has planted sympathies that shall live forever in the memory of the world, whose brilliant talents shone in the display of natural things, so that the most cultivated, whose powers shone with equal lustre, were not able to prepare mantles to cover the burning elements of an uncivilized world. What, then, shall we cease to mention the mighty of the earth, the noble work of God?

Yet those purer virtues remain untold. Those noble traits that marked the wild man's course lie buried in the shades of night; and who shall stand? I appeal to the lovers of liberty. But those few remaining descendants who now remain as the monument of the cruelty of those who came to improve our race, and correct our errors; and as the immortal Washington lives endeared and engraven on the hearts of every white in America, never to be forgotten in time,—even such is the immortal Philip honored, as held in memory by the degraded, but yet grateful descendants, who appreciate his character; so will every patriot, especially in this enlightened age, respect the rude yet all-accomplished son of the forest, that died a martyr to his cause, though unsuccessful, yet as glorious as the *American* Revolution. Where, then, shall we place the hero of the wilderness?

Justice and humanity for the remaining few prompt me to vindicate the character of him who yet lives in their hearts, and, if possible, melt the prejudice that exists in the hearts of those who are in the possession of his soil, and only by the right of conquest—is the aim of him who proudly tells you, the blood of a denominated savage runs in his veins. It is, however, true, that there are many who are said to be honorable warriors, who, in the wisdom of their civilized legislation, think it no crime to reek their vengeance upon whole nations and communities, until the fields are covered with blood, and the rivers turned into purple fountains, while groans, like distant thunder, are heard from the wounded, and the tens of thousands of the dying, leaving helpless families depending on their cares and sympathies for life; while a loud response is heard floating through the air from the ten thousand Indian children and orphans, who are left to mourn the honorable acts of a few—civilized men.

Now, if we have common sense and ability to allow the difference between the civilized and the uncivilized, we cannot but see that one mode of warfare is as just as the other; for, while one is sanctioned by authority of the enlightened and cultivated men, the other is an agreement according to the pure laws of nature, growing out of natural consequences; for nature always has her defence for every beast of the field; even the reptiles of the earth and the fishes of the sea have their weapons of war. But though frail man was made for a nobler purpose,—to live, to love and adore his God, and do good to his brother; for this reason, and this alone, the GOD of heaven prepared ways and means to blast anger, man's destroyer, and cause the Prince of Peace to rule, that man might swell those blessed notes, My image is of God, I am not a beast.

But as all men are governed by animal passions who are void of the true principles of GOD, whether cultivated or uncultivated, we shall now lay before you the true character of PHILIP, in relation to those hostilities between himself and the whites, and in so doing permit me to be plain and candid.

The first inquiry is, Who is PHILIP? He was the descendant of one of the most celebrated chiefs in the known world, for peace and universal benevolence towards all men; for injuries upon injuries, and the most daring robberies and barbarous deeds of death that were ever committed by the American Pilgrims, were with patience and resignation borne, in a manner that would do justice to any Christian nation or being in the world,—especially when we realize that it was voluntary suffering on the part of the good old chief. His country extensive—his men numerous, so as the wilderness was enlivened by them, say a thousand to one of the white men, and they, also, sick and feeble—where, then, shall we find one nation submitting so tamely to another, with such a host at their command? For injuries of much less magnitude have the people called Christians slain their brethren, till they could sing, like Sampson, With a jaw bone of an ass have we slain our thousands, and laid them in heaps. It will be well for us to lay those deeds and depredations committed by whites upon Indians, before the civilized world, and then they can judge for themselves.

It appears from history that in 1614, "There came one Henry Harley unto me, bringing with him a native of the Island of Capawick, a place at the south of Cape Cod, whose name was Epenuel. This man was taken upon the main by force, with some twenty-nine others," very probably good old Massasoit's men—see Harlow's Voyage, 1611, "by a ship, and carried to London, and from thence to be sold for slaves among the Spaniards; but the Indians being too shrewd, or, as they say, unapt for their use, they refused to traffic in Indians' blood and bones." This inhuman act of the whites caused the Indians to be jealous forever afterwards, which the white man acknowledges upon the first pages of the history of his country. (See Drake's Hist. of the Indians, page 7.)

How inhuman it was in those wretches, to come into a country where nature shone in beauty, spreading her wings over the vast continent, sheltering beneath her shades those natural sons of an Almighty Being, that shone in grandeur and lustre like stars of the first magnitude in the heavenly world; whose virtues far surpassed their more enlightened foes, notwithstanding their pretended zeal for religion and virtue. How they could go to work to enslave a free people, and call it religion, is beyond the power of my imagination, and out-strips the revelation of God's word. Oh, thou pretended hypocritical Christian, whoever thou art, to say it was the design of God, that we should murder and slay one another, because we have the power. Power was not given us to abuse each other, but a mere power delegated to us by the King of heaven, a weapon of defence against error and evil; and when abused, it will turn to our destruction. Mark, then, the history of nations throughout the world.

But notwithstanding the transgression of this power to destroy the Indians at their first discovery, yet it does appear that the Indians had a wish to be friendly. When the pilgrims came among them, (IYANOUGH's men,) there appeared an old woman, breaking out in solemn lamentations, declaring one Capt. Hunt had carried off three of her children, and they would never return here. The pilgrims replied, that they were bad and wicked men, but they were going to do better, and would never injure them at all. And to pay the poor mother, gave her a few brass trinkets, to atone for her three sons, and appease her present feelings, a woman nearly one hundred years of age. Oh, white woman! what would you think, if some foreign nation, unknown to you, should come and carry away from you three lovely children, whom you had dandled on the knee, and at some future time you should behold them, and break forth in sorrow, with your heart broken, and merely ask, sirs, where are my little ones, and some one should reply, it was passion, great passion; what would you think of them? Should you not think they were beings made more like rocks than men. Yet these same men came to these Indians for support, and acknowledge themselves, that no people could be used better than they were; that their treatment would do honor to any nation; that their provisions were in abundance; that they gave them venison, and sold them many hogsheads of corn to fill their stores, besides beans. This was in the year 1622. Had it not been for this humane act of the Indians, every white man would have been swept from the New England colonies. In their sickness too, the Indians were as tender to them as to their own children; and for all this, they were denounced as savages by those who had received all the acts of kindness they possibly could show them. After these social acts of the Indians towards those who were suffering, and those of their countrymen, who well knew the care their brethren had received by them: how were the Indians treated before that? Oh, hear! In the following manner, and their own words, we presume, they will not deny.

December, (O. S.) 1620, the pilgrims landed at Plymouth, and without asking liberty from any one, they possessed themselves of a portion of the country, and built themselves houses, and then made a treaty, and commanded them to accede to it. This, if now done, would be called an insult, and every white man would be called to go out and act the part of a patriot, to defend their country's rights; and if every intruder were butchered, it would be sung upon every hill-top in the Union, that victory and patriotism was the order of the day. And yet the Indians, (though many were dissatisfied,) without the shedding of blood, or imprisoning any one, bore it. And yet for their kindness and resignation towards the whites, they were called savages, and made by God on purpose for them to destroy. We might say, God understood his work better than this. But to proceed, it appears that a treaty was made by the pilgrims and the Indians, which treaty was kept during forty years; the young chiefs during this time, was showing the pilgrims how to live in their country, and find support for their wives and little ones; and for all this, they were receiving the applauses of being savages. The two gentlemen chiefs were Squanto and Samoset, that were so good to the pilgrims.

The next we present before you are things very appalling. We turn our attention to dates, 1623, January and March, when Mr. Weston

Colony, came very near starving to death; some of them were obliged to hire themselves to the Indians, to become their servants, in order that they might live. Their principal work was to bring wood and water; but not being contented with this, many of the whites sought to steal the Indian's corn; and because the Indians complained of it, and through their complaint, some one of their number being punished, as they say, to appease the savages. Now let us see who the greatest savages were; the person that stole the corn was a stout athletic man, and because of this, they wished to spare him, and take an old man who was lame and sickly, and that used to get his living by weaving, and because they thought he would not be of so much use to them, he was, although innocent of any crime, hung in his stead. Oh, savage, where art thou, to weep over the Christian's crimes. Another act of humanity for Christians, as they call themselves, that one Capt. Standish, gathering some fruit and provisions, goes forward with a black and hypocritical heart, and pretends to prepare a feast for the Indians; and when they sit down to eat, they seize the Indian's knives hanging about their necks, and stab them to the heart. The white people call this stabbing, feasting the savages. We suppose it might well mean themselves, their conduct being more like savages than Christians. They took one Wittumumet, the Chief's head, and put it upon a pole in their fort; and for aught we know, gave praise to their God for success in murdering a poor Indian; for we know it was their usual course to give praise to God for this kind of victory, believing it was God's will and command, for them to do so. We wonder if these same Christians do not think it the command of God, that they should lie, steal, and get drunk, commit fornication and adultery. The one is as consistent as the other. What say you, judges, is it not so, and was it not according as they did? Indians think it is.

But we will proceed to show another inhuman act. The whites robbed the Indian graves, and their corn, about the year 1632, which caused CHICATAUBUT to be displeased, who was chief, and also a son to the woman that was dead. And according to the Indian custom it was a righteous act to be avenged of the dead. Accordingly he called all his men together, and addressed them thus: "When last the glorious light of the sky was underneath this globe, and birds grew silent, I began to settle, as is my custom, to take repose. Before my eyes were fast closed, methought I saw a vision, at which my spirit was much troubled. A spirit cried aloud, Behold, my son, whom I have cherished, see the paps that gave thee suck, the hands that clasped thee warm, and fed thee oft. Can thou forget to take revenge of those wild people that have my monument defaced in a despiteful manner, disdaining our ancient antiquities and honorable customs? See, now, the Sachem's grave lies, like unto the common people of ignoble race, defaced. Thy mother doth complain, and implores thy aid against these thievish people, now come hither. If this be suffered, I shall not rest quiet within my everlasting habitation." War was the result. And where is there a people in the world that would see their friends robbed of their common property, their nearest and dearest friends; robbed, after their last respects to them? I appeal to you, who value your friends, and affectionate mothers, if you would have them robbed of their fine marble, and your storehouses broken open, without calling those to account, who did it? I trow not; and if another nation should come to these regions, and begin to rob and plunder all that came in their way, would not the orators of the day be called to address the people, and arouse them to war, for such insults? and, for all this, would they not be called Christians and patriots? Yes, it would be rung from Georgia to Maine, from the Ocean to the lakes, what fine men and Christians there were in the land. But when a few red children attempt to defend their rights, they are condemned as savages, by those, if possible, who have indulged in wrongs more cruel than the Indians.

But there is still more. In 1619 a number of Indians went on board of a ship, by order of their chief, and the whites set upon them, and murdered them without mercy; says Mr. Dermer, "without the Indians giving them the least provocation whatever." Is this insult to be borne, and not a word to be said? Truly, Christians would never bear it; why, then, think it strange that the denominated savages do not? Oh, thou white Christian, look at acts that honored your countrymen, to the destruction of thousands, for much less insults than that. And who, my dear sirs, were wanting of the name of savages—whites, or Indians? Let justice answer.

But we have more to present; and that is, the violation of a treaty that the Pilgrims proposed for the Indians to subscribe to, and they the first to break it. The Pilgrims promised to deliver up every transgressor of the Indian treaty, to them, to be punished according to their laws, and the Indians were to do likewise. Now it appears that an Indian had committed treason, by conspiring against the king's life, which is punishable with death; and Massasoit makes demand for the transgressor, and the Pilgrims refuse to give him up, although by their oath of alliance they had promised to do so. Their reasons were, he was beneficial to them. This shows how grateful they were to their former safeguard, and ancient protector. Now, who would have blamed this venerable old chief if he had declared war at once, and swept the whole colonies away? It was certainly in his power to do it, if he pleased; but no, he forbore, and forgave the whites. But where is there a people, called civilized, that would do it? we presume, none; and we doubt not but the Pilgrims would have exerted all their powers to be avenged, and to appease their ungodly passions. But it will be seen that this good old chief exercised more Christian forbearance than any of the governors of that age, or since. It might well be said he was a pattern for the Christians themselves; but by the Pilgrims he is denounced, as being a savage.

It does not appear that MASSASOIT or his sons were respected because they were human beings, but because they feared him; and we are led to believe that if it had been in the power of the Pilgrims, they would have butchered them out and out notwithstanding all the piety they professed. Only look for a few moments at the abuses the son of MASSASOIT received. ALEXANDER being sent for with armed men, and while he and his men were breaking their fast in the morning, they were taken immediately away, by order of the governor, without the least provocation, but merely through suspicion. ALEXANDER and his men saw them, and might have prevented it, but did not, saying the governor had no occasion to treat him in this manner; and the heartless wretch informed him that he would murder him upon the spot, if he did not go with him, presenting a sword at his breast; and had it not been for one of his men he would have yielded himself up upon the spot. ALEXANDER was a man of strong passion, and of a firm mind; and this insulting treatment of him caused him to fall sick of a fever, so that he never recovered. Some of the Indians were suspicious that he was poisoned to death. He died in the year 1662. "After him," says that eminent divine, Dr. Mather, "there rose up one PHILIP, of cursed memory." Perhaps if the Dr. was present, he would find that the memory of PHILIP was as far before his, in the view of sound, judicious men, as the sun is before the stars, at noonday. But we might suppose that men like Dr. Mather, so well versed in Scripture, would have known his work better than to have spoken evil of any one, or have cursed any of GOD's works. He ought to have known that GOD did not make his red children for him to curse; but if he wanted them cursed, he could have done it himself. But, on the contrary, his suffering Master commanded him to love his enemies, and to pray for his persecutors, and to do unto others as he would that men should do unto him. Now, we wonder if the sons of the Pilgrims would like to have us, poor Indians, come out and curse the Doctor, and all their sons, as we have been, by many of them. And suppose that, in some future day, our children should repay all these wrongs, would it not be doing as we, poor Indians, have been done to? But we sincerely hope there is more humanity in us, than that.

In the history of MASSASOIT we find that his own head men were not satisfied with the Pilgrims; that they looked upon them to be intruders, and had a wish to expel those intruders out of their coast; and no wonder that from the least reports the Pilgrims were ready to take it up. A false report was made respecting one TISQUANTUM, that he was murdered by an Indian, one of COUBANTANT's men. Upon this news, one Standish, a vile and malicious fellow, took fourteen of his lewd Pilgrims with him, and at midnight, when a deathless silence reigned throughout the wilderness; not even a bird is heard to send forth her sweet songs to charm and comfort those children of the woods; but all had taken their rest, to commence anew on the rising of the glorious sun. But to their sad surprise there was no rest for them, but they were surrounded by ruffians and assassins; yes, assassins; what better name can be given them? At that late hour of the night, meeting a house in the wilderness, whose inmates were nothing but a few helpless females and children; soon a voice is heard—Move not, upon the peril of your life. I appeal to this audience if there was any righteousness in their proceedings? Justice would say no. At the same time some of the females were so frightened, that some of them undertook to make their escape, upon which they were fired upon. Now it is doubtless the case that these females never saw a white man before, or ever heard a gun fired. It must have sounded to them like the rumbling of thunder, and terror must certainly have filled all their hearts. And can it be supposed that these innocent Indians could have looked upon them as good and trusty men? Do you look upon the midnight robber and assassin as being a Christian, and trusty man? These Indians had not done one single wrong act to the whites, but were as innocent of any crime, as any beings in the world. And do you believe that Indians cannot feel and see, as well as white people? If you think so, you are mistaken. Their power of feeling and knowing is as quick as yours. Now this is to be borne, as the pilgrims did as their Master told them to; but what color he was I leave it. But if the real sufferers say one word, they are denounced, as being wild and savage beasts.

But let us look a little further. It appears that in 1630, a benevolent Chief bid the pilgrims welcome to his shores; and in June 28, 1630, ceded his land to them for the small sum of eighty dollars, now Ipswich, Rowley, and a part of Essex. The following year, at the July term, 1631, these pilgrims of the new world, passed an act in court, that the friendly chief should not come into their houses short of paying fifty dollars, or an equivalent, that is ten beaver skins. Who could have supposed that the meek and lowly followers of virtue would have taken such methods to rob honest men of the woods. But for this insult, the pilgrims had well nigh lost their lives and their all, had it not been prevented by Robbin, an Indian, who apprized them of their danger. And now let it be understood, notwithstanding all the bitter feelings the whites have generally shown towards Indians, yet they have been the only instrument in preserving their lives.

The history of New England writers say, that our tribes were large and respectable. How then, could it be otherwise, but their safety rested in the hands of friendly Indians. In 1647, the pilgrims speak of large and respectable tribes. But let us trace them for a few moments. How have they been destroyed, is it by fair means? No. How then? By hypocritical proceedings, by being duped and flattered; flattered by informing the Indians that their God was a going to speak to them, and then place them before the cannon's mouth in a line, and then putting the match to it and kill thousands of them. We might suppose that meek Christians had better gods and weapons than cannon; weapons that were not carnal, but mighty through God, to the pulling down of strong holds. These are the weapons that modern Christians profess to have; and if the pilgrims did not have them, they ought not to be honored as such. But let us again review their weapons, to civilize the nations of this soil. What were they: rum and powder, and ball, together with all the diseases, such as the small pox, and every other disease immaginable; and in this way sweep off thousands and tens of thousands. And then it has been said, that these men who were free from these things, that they could not live among civilized people. We wonder how a virtuous people could live in a sink of diseases, a people who had never been used to them.

And who is to account for those destructions upon innocent families and helpless children. It was said by some of the New England writers, that living babes were found at the breast of their dead mothers. What an awful sight! and to think too, that these diseases were carried among them on purpose to destroy them. Let the children of the pilgrims blush, while the son of the forest drops a tear, and groans over the fate of his murdered and departed fathers. He would say to the sons of the pilgrims, (as Job said about his birth day,) let the day be dark, the 22d of December, 1622; let it be forgotten in your celebration, in your speeches, and by the burying of the Rock that your fathers first put their foot upon. For be it remembered, although the gospel is said to be glad tidings to all people, yet we poor Indians never have found those who brought it as messengers of mercy, but contrawise. We say, therefore, let every man of color wrap himself in mourning, for the 22d of December and the 4th of July are days of mourning and not of joy. (I would here say, there is an error in my book; it speaks of the 25th of December, but it should be the 22d. See Indian Nullification.) Let them rather fast and pray to the great Spirit, the Indian's God, who deals out mercy to his red children, and not destruction.

Oh, Christians, can you answer for those beings that have been destroyed by your hostilities, and beings too that lies endeared to God as yourselves? his Son being their Saviour as well as yours, and alike to all men? And will you presume to say that you are executing the judgments of God by so doing, or as many really are approving the works of their fathers to be genuine, as it is certain that every time they celebrate the day of the pilgrims they do? Although in words they deny it, yet in works they approve of the iniquities of their fathers. And as the seed of iniquity and prejudice was sown in that day, so it still remains; and there is a deep rooted popular opinion in the hearts of many, that Indians were made, &c. on purpose for destruction, to be driven out by white Christians, and they to take their places; and that God had decreed it from all eternity. If such theologians would only study the works of nature more, they would understand the purposes of good better than they do. That the favor of the Almighty was good and holy, and all his nobler works were made to adorn his image, by being his grateful servants, and admiring each other as angels; and not as they say, to drive and devour each other. And that you may know the spirit of the pilgrims yet remain, we will present before you the words of a humble divine of the far West. He says, "the desert becomes an Eden." Rev. NAHUM GOLD, of Union Grove, Putman, writes under date June 12, 1835, says he, "let any man look at this settlement, and reflect what it was three years ago, and his heart can but kindle up while he exclaims, 'what has God wrought!' the savage has left the ground for civilized man; the rich prairie, from bringing forth all its strengths to be burned, is now receiving numerous enclosures, and brings a harvest of corn and wheat to feed the church. Yes, sir, this is now God's vineyard; he has gathered the vine, the choice vine, and brought it from a far country, and has planted it on a goodly soil. He expects fruit now. He gathered out the stones thereof, and drove the red Canaanites from trampling it down, or in any way hindering its increase."—*N. Y. Evangelist, August* 1.

But what next should we hear from this very pious man. Why, my brethren, the poor missionaries want money to go and convert the poor heathen, as if God could not convert them where they were; but must first drive them out. If God wants the red men converted, we should think he could do it as well in one place as in another. But must I say, and shall I say it, that missionaries have injured us more than they have done us good, by degrading us as a people, in breaking up our governments, and leaving us without any suffrages whatever, or a legal right among men. Oh, what cursed doctrine is this, it most certainly is not fit to civilize men with, much more to save their souls; and we poor Indians want no such missionaries around us. But I would suggest one thing, and that is, let the ministers and people use the colored people they have already around them, like human beings, before they go to convert any more; and let them show it in their churches; and let them proclaim it upon the house tops, and I would say to the benevolent, withhold your hard earnings from them, unless they do do it; until they can stop laying their own wickedness to God, which is blasphemy.

But if God was like his subjects, we should all have been swept off before now; for we find that of late, pilgrims' children have got to killing and mobbing each other, as they have got rid of most all the Indians. This is worse than my countrymen ever did; for they never mobbed one another, and I was in hopes that the sons of the pilgrims had improved a little. But the more honorable may thank their fathers for such a spirit in this age. And remember that their walls of prejudice was built with untempered mortar, contrary to God's command; and be assured, it will fall upon their children, though I sincerely hope they will not be seriously injured by it. Although I myself, now and then feel a little of its pressure, as though I should not be able to sustain the shock; but I trust the great Spirit will stand by me, as also good and honorable men will, being as it were the last, still lingering upon the shores of time, standing as it were upon the graves of his much injured race, to plead their cause, and speak for the rights of the remaining few. Although it is said by many, that Indians had no rights, neither do they regard their rights; nor can they look a white man in the face, and ask him for them. If the white man did but know it, the Indians knows it would do no good to spend his breath for nought. But if we can trust to Roger Williams' word, in regard to Indian rights: he says, no people were more so; that the cause of all their wars were about their hunting grounds. And it is certain their boundaries were set to their respective tribes; so that each one knew his own range. The poet speaks thus of Canonicus, in 1803:

> *Almighty Prince, of venerable age,*
> *A fearless warrior, but of peace the friend;*
> *His breast a treasury of maxims sage,*
> *His arm a host, to punish or defend.*

It was said he was eighty-four years of age when he died, an able defender of his rights. Thus it does appear that Indians had rights, and those rights were near and dear to them, as your stores and farms, and firesides are to the whites, and their wives and children also. And how the pilgrims could rejoice at their distresses, I know not; what divinity men were made of in those days, rather puzzles me now and then. Now, for example, we will lay before you the conduct of an Indian and the whites, and leave you, dear sirs, to judge.

History informs us that in Kennebunk there lived an Indian, remarkable for his good conduct, and who received a grant of land from the State, and fixed himself in a new township, where a number of white families were settled. Though not ill-treated, yet the common prejudices against Indians prevented any sympathy with him, though he himself did all that lay in his power to comfort his white neighbors, in case of sickness and death. But now let us see the scene reversed. This poor Indian, that had nourished, and waited to aid the Pilgrims in their trouble, now vainly looks for help, when sickness and death comes into his family. Hear his own words. He speaks to the inhabitants thus: "When white man's child die, Indian man he sorry; he help bury him. When my child die, no one speak to me; I make his grave alone. I can no live here." He gave up his farm, dug up the body of his child, and carried it 200 miles, through the wilderness, to join the Canadian

Indians. What dignity there was in this man; and we do not wonder that he felt so indignant at the proceedings of the then called Christians. But this was as they were taught by their haughty divines and orators of the day. But, nevertheless, the people were to blame, for they might have read for themselves; and they doubtless would have found that we were not made to be vessels of wrath, as they say we were. And had the whites found it out, perhaps they would not have rejoiced at a poor Indian's death; or when they were swept off, would not have called it the Lord killing the Indians to make room for them upon their lands. This is something like many people wishing for their friends to die, that they might get their property. I am astonished when I look at peoples' absurd blindness—when all are liable to die, and all subject to all kinds of diseases. For example; why is it that epidemics have raged so much among the more civilized? in London, 1660, the plague; and in 1830 and 1831, the cholera, in the old and new world, when the inhabitants were lain in heaps by that epidemic. Should I hear of an Indian rejoicing over the inhabitants, I would no longer own him as a brother. But, dear friends, you know that no Indian knew by the Bible it was wrong to kill, because he knew not the Bible, and its sacred laws. But it is certain the Pilgrims knew better than to break the commands of their Lord and Master; they knew that it was written, "thou shalt not kill."

But having laid a mass of history and exposition before you, the purpose of which is to show that Philip and all the Indians generally, felt indignantly towards whites, whereby they were more easily allied together by Philip, their King and Emperor, we come to notice more particularly his history. As to his Majesty, King Philip, it was certain that his honor was put to the test, and it was certainly to be tried, even at the loss of his life and country. It is a matter of uncertainty about his age; but his birth-place was at Mount Hope, Rhode Island, where Massasoit, his father lived, till 1656, and died, as also his brother, Alexander, by the governor's ill-treating him, (that is, Winthrop,) which caused his death, as before mentioned, in 1662; after which, the kingdom fell into the hands of Philip, the greatest man that ever lived upon the American shores. Soon after his coming to the throne, it appears he began to be noticed, though, prior to this, it appears that he was not forward in the councils of war or peace. When he came into office it appears that he knew there was great responsibility resting upon himself and country; that it was likely to be ruined by those rude intruders around him; though he appears friendly, and is willing to sell them lands for almost nothing, as we shall learn from dates of the Plymouth Colony, which commence June 23, 1664. William Benton, of Rhode Island, a merchant, buys Matapoisett of PHILIP and wife, but no sum is set, which he gave for it. To this deed, his counsellors, and wife, and two of the Pilgrims, were witnesses. In 1665 he sold New Bedford and Compton for forty dollars. In 1667 he sells to Constant Southworth and others all the meadow lands from Dartmouth to Matapoisett, for which he received sixty dollars. The same year he sells to Thomas Willet a tract of land two miles in length, and perhaps the same in width, for which he received forty dollars. In 1668 he sold a tract of some square miles, now called Swanzey. The next year he sells five hundred acres in Swanzey, for which he received eighty dollars. His counsellors and interpreters, with the Pilgrims, were witnesses to these deeds.

OSAMEQUAN, for valuable considerations, in the year 1641 sold to John Brown and Edward Winslow a tract of land eight miles square, situated on both sides of Palmer's River. PHILIP, in 1668 was required to sign a quit-claim of the same, which we understand he did in the presence of his counsellors. In the same year PHILIP laid claim to a portion of land called New Meadows, alleging that it was not intended to be conveyed in a former deed, for which Mr. Brown paid him forty-four dollars, in goods; so it was settled without difficulty. Also, in 1669, for forty dollars he sold to one John Cook, a whole island, called Nokatay, near Dartmouth. The same year PHILIP sells a tract of land in Middleborough for fifty-two dollars. In 1671 he sold to Hugh Cole a large tract of land, lying near Swanzey, for sixteen dollars. In 1672 he sold sixteen square miles to William Breton and others, of Taunton, for which he and his chief received five hundred and seventy-two dollars. This contract, signed by himself and chiefs, ends the sales of lands with PHILIP, for all which he received nine hundred and seventy-four dollars, as far as we can learn by the records.

Here PHILIP meets with a most bitter insult, in 1673, from one Peter Talmon, of Rhode Island, who complained to the Plymouth Court against PHILIP, of Mount Hope, predecessor, heir, and administrator of his brother ALEXANDER, deceased, in an action on the case, to the damage of three thousand and two hundred dollars, for which the Court gave verdict in favor of Talmon, the young Pilgrim; for which PHILIP had to make good to the said Talmon a large tract of land at Sapamet and other places adjacent; and for the want thereof, that is, more land that was not taken up, the complainant is greatly damnified. This is the language in the Pilgrims' Court. Now let us review this a little. The man who bought this land made the contract, as he says, with Alexander, ten or twelve years before; then why did he not bring forward his contract before the Court? It is easy to understand why he did not. Their object was to cheat, or get the whole back again in this way. Only look at the sum demanded, and it is enough to satisfy the critical observer. This course of proceedings caused the Chief and his people to entertain strong jealousies of the whites.

In the year 1668 Philip made a complaint against one Weston, who had wronged one of his men of a gun and some swine; and we have no account that he got any justice for his injured brethren. And, indeed, it would be a strange thing for poor unfortunate Indians to find justice in those Courts of the pretended pious, in those days, or even since; and for a proof of my assertion I will refer the reader or hearer to the records of Legislatures and Courts throughout New England; and also to my book, Indian Nullification.

We would remark still further; who stood up in those days, and since, to plead Indian rights? Was it the friend of the Indian? No; it was his enemies who rose; his enemies, to judge and pass sentence. And we know that such kind of characters as the Pilgrims were, in regard to the Indians' rights, who, as they say, had none, must certainly always give verdict against them, as, generally speaking, they always have. Prior to this insult it appears that Philip had met with great difficulty with the Pilgrims; that they appeared to be suspicious of him in 1671; and the Pilgrims sent for him, but he did not appear to move as though he cared much for their messenger, which caused them to be still more suspicious. What grounds the Pilgrims had is not ascertained, unless it is attributed to a guilty conscience for wrongs done to Indians. It appears that Philip, when he got ready, goes near to them, and sends messengers to Taunton, to invite the Pilgrims to come and treat with him; but the governor being either too proud, or afraid, sends messengers to him to come to their residence at Taunton, to which he complied. Among these messengers was the Honorable Roger Williams, a Christian and a patriot, and a friend to the Indians, for which we rejoice. Philip, not liking to trust the Pilgrims, left some of the whites in his stead, to warrant his safe return. When Philip and his men had come near the place, some of the Plymouth people were ready to attack him; this rashness was, however, prevented by the Commissioner of

Massachusetts, who met there with the Governor, to treat with Philip; and it was agreed upon to meet in the meetinghouse. Philip's complaint was, that the Pilgrims had injured the planting grounds of his people. The Pilgrims acting as umpires say the charges against them were not sustained; and because it was not, to their satisfaction, the whites wanted that Philip should order all his men to bring in his arms and ammunition; and the Court was to dispose of them as they pleased. The next thing was, that Philip must pay the cost of the treaty, which was four hundred dollars. The Pious Dr. Mather says, that Philip was appointed to pay a sum of money to defray the charges that his insolent clamors had put the Colony to. We wonder if the Pilgrims were as ready to pay the Indians for the trouble they put them to. If they were, it was with the instruments of death. It appears that Philip did not wish to make war with them, but compromised with them; and in order to appease the Pilgrims he actually did order his men, whom he could not trust, to deliver them up; but his own men withheld, with the exception of a very few.

Now what an unrighteous act this was in the people, who professed to be friendly and humane, and peaceable to all men. It could not be that they were so devoid of sense as to think these illiberal acts would produce peace; but contrawise, continual broils. And in fact it does appear that they courted war instead of peace, as it appears from a second council that was held by order of the Governor, at Plymouth, September 13, 1671. It appears that they sent again for PHILIP; but he did not attend, but went himself and made complaint to the governor, which made him write to the council, and ordered them to desist, to be more mild, and not to take such rash measures. But it appears that on the 24th, the scene changed; that they held another council, and the disturbers of the peace, the intruders upon a peaceable people, say they find PHILIP guilty of the following charges:

1. That he had neglected to bring in his arms, although competent time had been given him.

2. That he had carried insolently and proudly towards us on several occasions, in refusing to come down to our courts, (when sent for,) to procure a right understanding betwixt us.

What an insult this was to his Majesty, and independent Chief of a powerful nation, should come at the beck and call of his neighbors whenever they pleased to have him do it. Besides, did not PHILIP do as he agreed, at Taunton, that is in case there was more difficulty they were to leave it to Massachusetts, to be settled there in the high council, and both parties were to abide by their decision; but did the Pilgrims wait? No. But being infallible, of course they could not err.

The third charge was, harboring divers Indians not his own men; but vagabond Indians.

Now what a charge this was to bring against a King, calling his company vagabonds, because it did not happen to please them; and what right had they to find fault with his company. I do not believe that PHILIP ever troubled himself about the white people's company, and prefer charges against them for keeping company with whom they pleased. Neither do I believe he called their company vagabonds, for he was more noble than that.

The fourth charge is, that he went to Massachusetts with his council, and complained against them, and turned their brethren against them.

This was more a complaint against themselves than Philip, inasmuch it represents that Philip's story was so correct, that they were blameable.

5. That he had not been quite so civil as they wished him to be.

We presume that Philip felt himself much troubled by these intruders, and of course put them off from time to time, or did not take much notice of their proposals. Now such charges as those, we think are to no credit of the pilgrims. However, this council ended much as the other did, in regard to disarming the Indians, which they never were able to do. Thus ended the events of 1671.

But it appears that the pilgrims could not be contented with what they had done, but they must send an Indian, and a traitor, to preach to Philip and his men, in order to convert him and his people to Christianity. The preacher's name was Sassamon. I would appeal to this audience, is it not certain that the Plymouth people strove to pick a quarrel with Philip and his men. What could have been more insulting than to send a man to them who was false, and looked upon as such; for it is most certain that a traitor was above all others, the more to be detested than any other. And not only so, it was the laws of the Indians, that such a man must die; that he had forfeited his life; and when he made his appearance among them, Philip would have killed him upon the spot, if his council had not persuaded him not to. But it appears that in March, 1674, one of Philip's men killed him, and placed him beneath the ice in a certain pond near Plymouth; doubtless by the order of Philip. After this, search was made for him, and he found there a certain Indian, by the name of Patuckson; Tobias, also, his son were apprehended and tried. Tobias was one of Philip's counsellors, as it appears from the records that the trial did not end here, that it was put over, and that two of the Indians entered into bonds for $400, for the appearance of Tobias at the June term; for which a mortgage of land was taken to that amount, for his safe return. June having arrived, three instead of one are arraigned. There was no one but Tobias suspected at the previous Court. Now two others are arraigned, tried, condemned and executed, (making three in all,) in June the 8th, 1675, by hanging and shooting. It does not appear that any more than one was guilty, and it was said that he was known to acknowledge it; but the other two persisted in their innocency to the last.

This murder of the preacher brought on the war a year sooner than it was anticipated by Philip. But this so exasperated King Philip, that from that day he studied to be revenged of the pilgrims; judging that his white intruders had nothing to do in punishing his people for any crime, and that it was in violation of treaties of ancient date. But when we look at this, how bold and how daring it was to Philip, as though they would bid defiance to him, and all his authority, we do not wonder at his exasperation. When the Governor finds that his Majesty was displeased, he then sends messengers to him, and wishes to know why he would make war upon him, (as if he had done all right,) and wished to enter into a new treaty with him. The King answered them thus: Your Governor is but a subject of King Charles of England, I shall not treat with a subject; I shall treat of peace only with a King, my brother; when he comes, I am ready.

This answer of Philip's to the messengers, is worthy of note throughout the world. And never could a prince answer with more dignity in regard to his official authority than he did; disdaining the idea of placing himself upon a par of the minor subjects of a King; letting them know at the same time, that he felt his independence more than they thought he did. And indeed it was time for him to wake up, for now the subjects of King Charles had taken one of his counsellors and killed him, and he could no longer trust them. Until the execution of these three Indians, supposed to be the murderers of Sassamon, no hostility was committed by Philip or his warriors. About the time of their trial, he was said to be marching his men up and down the country in arms; but when it was known, he could no longer restrain his young men, who, upon the 24th of June, provoked the people of Swansey, by killing their cattle and other injuries, which was a signal to commence the war, and what they had desired, as a superstitious notion prevailed among the Indians, that whoever fired the first gun of either party, would be conquered. Doubtless a notion they had received from the pilgrims. It was upon a fast day too, when the first gun was fired; and as the people were returning from church, they were fired upon by the Indians, when several of them were killed. It is not supposed that Philip directed this attack, but was opposed to it. Though it is not doubted that he meant to be revenged upon his enemies; for during some time he had been cementing his countrymen together, as it appears that he had sent to all the disaffected tribes, who also had watched the movements of the comers from the new world, and were as dissatisfied as Philip himself was with their proceedings.

> *Now around the council fires they meet,*
> *The young nobles for to greet;*
> *Their tales of wo and sorrows to relate,*
> *About the pilgrims, their wretched foes.*
>
> *And while their fires were blazing high,*
> *Their King and Emperor to greet;*
> *His voice like lightning fires their hearts,*
> *To stand the test or die.*
>
> *See those pilgrims from the world unknown,*
> *No love for Indians do know:*
> *Although our fathers fed them well*
> *With venison rich, of precious kinds.*
>
> *No gratitude to Indians now is shown,*
> *From people saved by them alone;*
> *All gratitude that poor Indians do know,*
> *Is, we are robbed of all our rights.*

At this council it appears that Philip made the following speech to his chiefs, counsellors and warriors:

BROTHERS,—You see this vast country before us, which the great Spirit gave to our fathers and us; you see the buffalo a d deer that now are our support.—Brothers, you see these little ones, our wives and children, who are looking to us for food and raiment; and you now see the foe before you, that they have grown insolent and bold; that all our ancient customs are disregarded; the treaties made by our fathers and us are broken, and all of us insulted; our council fires disregarded, and all the ancient customs of our fathers; our brothers murdered before our eyes, and their spirits cry to us for revenge. Brothers, these people from the unknown world will cut down our groves, spoil our hunting and planting grounds, and drive us and our children from the graves of our fathers, and our council fires, and enslave our women and children.

This famous speech of Philip was calculated to arouse them to arms, to do the best they could in protecting and defending their rights. The blow had now been struck, the die was cast, and nothing but blood and carnage was before them. And we find Philip as active as the wind, as dextrous as a giant, firm as the pillows of heaven, and as fierce as a lion, a powerful foe to contend with indeed: and as swift as an eagle, gathering together his forces, to prepare them for the battle. And as it would swell our address too full, to mention all the tribes in Philip's train of warriors, suffice it to say that from six to seven were with him at different times. When he begins the war, he goes forward and musters about 500 of his men, and arms them complete, and about 900 of the other, making in all about fourteen hundred warriors when he commenced. It must be recollected that this war was legally declared by Philip, so that the colonies had a fair warning. It was no savage war of surprise as some suppose, but one sorely provoked by the pilgrims themselves. But when Philip and his men fought, as they were accustomed to do, and according to their mode of war, it was no more than what could be expected. But we hear no particular acts of cruelty committed by Philip during the siege. But we find more manly nobility in him, than we do in all the head pilgrims put together, as we shall see during this quarrel between them. Philip's young men were eager to do exploits, and to lead captive their haughty lords. It does appear that every Indian heart had been lighted up at the council fires, at Philip's speech, and that the forest was literally alive with this injured race. And now town after town fell before them. The pilgrims with their forces were ever marching in one direction, while Philip and his forces were marching in another, burning all before them, until Middleborough, Taunton and Dartmouth were laid in ruins, and forsaken by its inhabitants.

At the great fight at Pocasset, Philip commanded in person, where he also was discovered with his host in a dismal swamp. He had retired here with his army to secure a safe retreat from the pilgrims, who were in close pursuit of him, and their numbers were so powerful they thought the fate of Philip was sealed. They surrounded the swamp, in hopes to destroy him and his army. At the edge of the swamp Philip had secreted a few of his men to draw them into ambush, upon which the pilgrims showed fight; Philip's men retreating and the whites pursuing them till they were surrounded by Philip, and nearly all cut off. This was a sorry time to them; the pilgrims, however, reinforced, but ordered a retreat, supposing it impossible for Philip to escape, and knowing his forces to be great, it was conjectured by some to build a fort to starve him out, as he had lost but few men in the fight. The situation of Philip was rather peculiar, as there was but one outlet to the swamp, and a river before him nearly seven miles to descend. The pilgrims placed a guard around the swamp for 13 days, which gave Philip and his men time to prepare canoes to make good his retreat; in which he did, to the Connecticut river, and in his retreat lost but fourteen men. We may look upon this move of Philip's to be equal, if not superior to that of Washington crossing the Delaware. For while Washington was assisted by all the knowledge that art and science could give, together with all the instruments of defence, and edged tools to prepare rafts, and the like helps for safety across the river, Philip was naked as to any of these things, possessing only what nature, his mother had bestowed upon him; and yet makes his escape with equal praise. But he would not even lost a man, had it not been for Indians who were hired to fight against Indians, with promise of their enjoying equal rights with their white brethren; but not one of those promises have as yet been fulfilled by the pilgrims or their children, though they must acknowledge, that without the aid of Indians and their guides, they must inevitably been swept off. It was only then by deception that the pilgrims gained the country, as their word has never been fulfilled in regard to Indian rights.

Philip having now taken possession of the back settlements of Massachusets, one town after another was swept off. A garrison being established at Northfield by the pilgrims, and while endeavoring to reinforce it with thirty-six armed, twenty out of their number was killed, and one taken prisoner. At the same time Philip so managed it as to cut off their retreat, and take their ammunition from them.

About the month of August, they took a young lad about fourteen years of age, whom they intended to make merry with the next day; but the pilgrims said God touched the Indians' heart, and they let him go. About the same time, the whites took an old man of Philip's, whom they found alone; and because he would not turn traitor, and inform them where Philip was, they pronounced him worthy of death; and by them was executed, cutting off first his arms and then his head. We wonder why God did not touch the pilgrims' heart, and save them from cruelty, as well as the Indians.

We would now notice an act in King Philip, that outweighs all the other princes and emperors in the world. That is, when his men began to be in want of money, having a coat neatly wrought with mampampeag, (*i. e.* Indian money,) he cut it to pieces, and distributed it among all his chiefs and warriors; it being better than the old continental money of the revolution, in Washington's day, as not one Indian soldier found fault with it, as we could ever learn; so that it cheered their hearts still to persevere to maintain their rights and expel their enemies.

On the 18th of September, the pilgrims made a tour from Hadley to Deerfield, with about eighty men, to bring their valuable articles of clothing and provisions. Having loaded their teams and returning, Philip and his men attacked them, and nearly slew them all. The attack was made near Sugar-loaf Hill. It was said that in this fight, the pilgrims lost their best men of Essex, and all their goods; upon which there were many made widows and orphans in one day. Philip now having done what he could upon the Western frontiers of Massachusetts, and believing his presence was wanted among his allies, the Narragansets, to keep them from being duped by the pilgrims, he is next known to be in their country.

The pilgrims determined to break down Philip's power, if possible, with the Narragansets: thus they raised an army of 1500 strong, to go against them and destroy them if possible. In this, Massachusetts, Plymouth and Connecticut all join in severally, to crush Philip. Accordingly in December, in 1675, the pilgrims set forward to destroy them. Preceding their march, Philip had made all arrangements for the winter, and had fortified himself beyond what was common for his countrymen to do, upon a small island near South Kingston, R. I. Here he intended to pass the winter with his warriors, and their wives and children. About 500 Indian houses was erected of a superior kind, in which was deposited all their stores, tubs of corn, and other things, piled up to a great height, which rendered it bullet proof. It was supposed that about 3000 persons had taken up their residence in it. (I would remark, that Indians took better care of themselves in those days than they have been able to since.) Accordingly on the 19th day of December, after the pilgrims had been out in the extreme cold, for nearly one month, lodging in tents, and their provision being short, and the air full of snow, they had no other alternative than to attack Philip in the fort. Treachery however, hastened his ruin; one of his men by hope of reward from the deceptive pilgrims, betrayed his country into their hands. The traitor's name was Peter. No white man was acquainted with the way, and it would have been almost impossible for them to have found it, much less to have captured it. There was but one point where it could have been entered or assailed with any success, and this was fortified much like a block house, directly in front of the entrance, and also flankers to cover a cross fire. Besides high palisides, an immense hedge of fallen trees of nearly a rod in thickness. Thus surrounded by trees and water, there was but one place that the pilgrims could pass. Nevertheless, they made the attempt. Philip now had directed his men to fire, and every platoon of the Indians swept every white man from the path one after another, until six captains, with a great many of the men had fallen. In the mean time, one Captain Moseley, with some of his men had some how or other gotten into the fort in another way, and surprised them; by which the pilgrims were enabled to capture the fort, at the same time setting fire to it, and hewing down men, women and children indiscriminately. Philip, however, was enabled to escape with many of his warriors. It is said at this battle eighty whites were killed, and one hundred and fifty wounded; many of whom died of their wounds afterwards, not being able to dress them till they had marched 18 miles; also leaving many of their dead in the fort. It is said that 700 of the Narragansets perished. The greater part of them being women and children.

It appears that God did not prosper them much after all. It is believed that the sufferings of the pilgrims were without a parallel in history; and it is supposed that the horrors and burning elements of Moscow, will bear but a faint resemblance of that scene. The thousands and tens of thousands assembled there with their well disciplined forces, bear but little comparison to that of modern Europe, when the inhabitants, science, manners and customs are taken into consideration. We might well admit the above fact, and say, the like was never known among any heathen nation in the world; for none but those worse than heathens, would have suffered so much, for the sake of being revenged upon those of their enemies. Philip had repaired to his quarters to take care of his people and not to have them exposed. We should not have wondered quite so much if Philip had gone forward and acted thus. But when a people, calling themselves Christians, conduct in this manner, we think they are censurable, and no pity at all ought to be had for them.

It appears that one of the whites had married one of Philip's countrymen; and they, the pilgrims, said he was a traitor, and therefore they said he must die. So they quartered him; and as history informs us, they said, he being a heathen, but a few tears were shed at his funeral. Here, then, because a man would not turn and fight against his own wife and family, or leave them, he was condemned as an heathen. We presume that no honest men will commend those ancient fathers, for such absurd conduct. Soon after this, Philip and his men left that part of the country, and retired farther back, near the Mohawks; where, in July 1676, some of his men were slain by the Mohawks. Notwithstanding this, he strove to get them to join him; and here it is said that Philip did not do that which was right; that he killed some of the Mohawks and laid it to the whites, in order that he might get them to join him. If so, we cannot consistently believe he did right. But he was so exasperated that nothing but revenge would satisfy him. All this act was no worse than our political men do in our days, of their strife to wrong each other, who profess to be enlightened; and all for the sake of carrying their points. Heathen-like, either by the sword, calumny or deception of every kind; and the late duels among the called high men of honor, is sufficient to warrant my statements. But while we pursue our history in regard to Philip, we find that he made many successful attempts against the pilgrims, in surprising and driving them from their posts, during the year 1676, in February, and through till August, in which time many of the Christian Indians joined him. It is thought by many, that all would have joined him, if they had been left to their choice, as it appears they did not like their white brethren very well. It appears that Philip treated his prisoners with a great deal more Christian-like spirit than the pilgrims did; even Mrs. Rolandson, although speaking with bitterness sometimes of the Indians, yet in her journal she speaks not a word against him. Philip even hires her to work for him, and pays her for her work, and then invites her to dine with him and to smoke with him. And we have many testimonies that he was kind to his prisoners; and when the English wanted to redeem Philip's prisoners, they had the privilege.

Now did Governor Winthrop, or any of those ancient divines use any of his men so? No. Was it known that they received any of their female captives into their houses and fed them? No; it cannot be found upon history. Were not the females completely safe, and none of them were violated, as they acknowledge themselves? But was it so when the Indian women fell into the hands of the pilgrims? No. Did the Indians get a chance to redeem their prisoners? No. But when they were taken, they were either compelled to turn traitors and join their enemies, or be butchered upon the spot. And this is the dishonest method that the famous Capt. Church used in doing his great exploits; and in no other way could he ever gained one battle. So after all, Church only owes his exploits to the honesty of the Indians, who told the truth, and to his own deceptive heart in duping them. Here it is to be understood, that the whites have always imposed upon the credulity of the Indians. It is with shame, I acknowledge, that I have to notice so much corruption of a people calling themselves Christians. If they were like my people, professing no purity at all, then their crimes would not appear to have such magnitude. But while they appear to be by profession more virtuous, their crimes still blacken. It makes them truly to appear to be like mountains filled with smoke; and thick darkness covering them all around.

But we have another dark and corrupt deed for the sons of the pilgrims to look at, and that is the fight and capture of Philip's son and wife, and many of his warriors, in which Philip lost about 130 men killed and wounded; this was in August 1676. But the most horrid act was in taking Philip's son, about ten years of age, and selling him to be a slave away from his father and mother. While I am writing, I can hardly restrain my feelings, to think a people calling themselves Christians, should conduct so scandalous, so outrageous, making themselves appear so despicable in the eyes of the Indians; and even now in this audience, I doubt not but there is men honorable enough to despise the conduct of those pretended Christians. And surely none but such as believe they did right, will ever go and undertake to celebrate that day of their landing, the 22d of December. Only look at it, then stop and pause. My fathers came here for liberty themselves, and then they must go and chain that mind, that image they professed to serve; not content to rob and cheat the poor ignorant Indians, but must take one of the King's sons, and make a slave of him. Gentlemen and ladies, I blush at these tales, if you do not, especially when they professed to be a free and humane people. Yes, they did; they took a part of my tribe, and sold them to the Spaniards in Bermuda, and many others; and then on the Sabbath day, these people would gather themselves together, and say that God is no respecter of persons; while the divines would pour forth, "he that says he loves God and hates his brother, is a liar, and the truth is not in him." And at the same time they hating and selling their fellow men in bondage. And there is no manner of doubt but that all my countrymen would have been enslaved if they had tamely submitted. But no sooner would they butcher every white man that come in their way, and even put an end to their own wives and children, and that was all that prevented them from being slaves; yes, *all*. It was not the good will of those holy pilgrims that prevented, no. But I would speak, and I could wish it might be like the voice of thunder, that it might be heard afar off, even to the ends of the earth. He that will advocate slavery, is worse than a beast, is a being devoid of shame; and has gathered around him the most corrupt and debasing principles in the world; and I care not whether he be a minister or member of any church in the world; no, not excepting the head men of the nation. And he that will not set his face against its corrupt principles, is a coward, and not worthy of being numbered among men and Christians. And conduct too that libels the laws of the country, and the word of God, that men profess to believe in.

After Philip had his wife and son taken, sorrow filled his heart; but notwithstanding, as determined as ever to be revenged, though was pursued by the duped Indians and Church, into a swamp; one of the men proposing to Philip that he had better make peace with the enemy, upon which he slew him upon the spot. And the pilgrims being also repulsed by Philip, were forced to retreat with the loss of one man in particular, whose name was Thomas Lucas, of Plymouth. We rather suspect that he was some related to Lucas and Hedge, who made their famous speeches against the poor Marshpees, in 1834, in the Legislature, in Boston, against freeing them from slavery, that their fathers, the pilgrims, had made of them for years.

Philip's forces had now become very small, so many having been duped away by the whites, and killed, that it was now easy surrounding him. Therefore, upon the 12th of August, Captain Church surrounded the swamp where Philip and his men had encamped, early in the morning, before they had risen, doubtless led on by an Indian who was either compelled or hired to turn traitor. Church had now placed his guard so that it was impossible for Philip to escape without being shot. It is doubtful, however, whether they would have taken him if he had not been surprised. Suffice it to say, however, this was the case. A sorrowful morning to the poor Indians, to lose such a valuable man. When coming out of the swamp, he was fired upon by an Indian, and killed dead upon the spot.

I rejoice that it was even so, that the Pilgrims did not have the pleasure of tormenting him. The white man's gun missing fire lost the honor of killing the truly great man, Philip. The place where Philip fell was very muddy. Upon this news, the Pilgrims gave three cheers; then Church ordering his body to be pulled out of the mud, while one of those tender-hearted Christians exclaims, what a dirty creature he looks like. And we have also Church's speech upon that subject, as follows: For as much as he has caused many a pilgrim to lie above ground unburied, to rot, not one of his bones shall be buried. With him fell five of his best and most trusty men; one the son of a chief, who fired the first gun in the war.

Captain Church now orders him to be cut up. Accordingly, he was quartered and hung up upon four trees; his head and one hand given to the Indian who shot him, to carry about to show. At which sight it so overjoyed the pilgrims, that they would give him money for it; and in this way obtained a considerable sum. After which, his head was sent to Plymouth, and exposed upon a gibbet for twenty years; and his hand to Boston, where it was exhibited in savage triumph; and his mangled body denied a resting place in the tomb, as thus adds the poet,

> "Cold with the beast he slew, he sleeps,
> O'er him no filial spirit weeps."

I think that as a matter of honor, that I can rejoice that no such evil conduct is recorded of the Indians; that they never hung up any of the white warriors, who were head men. And we add the famous speech of Dr. Increase Mather; he says, during the bloody contest, the pious fathers wrestled hard and long with their God, in prayer, that he would prosper their arms, and deliver their enemies into their hands. And when upon stated days of prayer, the Indians got the advantage, it was considered as a rebuke of divine providence, (we suppose the Indian prayed best then,) which stimulated them to more ardor. And on the contrary, when they prevailed, they considered it as an immediate interposition in their favor. The Doctor closes thus: Nor could they, the pilgrims, cease crying to the Lord against Philip, until they had prayed the bullet through his heart. And in speaking of the slaughter of Philip's people at Narraganset, he says, We have heard of two and twenty Indian captains slain, all of them, and brought down to hell in one day. Again, in speaking of a Chief who had sneered at the pilgrims' religion, and who had withal, added a most hideous blasphemy, Immediately upon which a bullet took him in the head, and dashed out his brains, sending his cursed soul in a moment among the devils and blasphemers in hell forever. It is true that this language is sickening, and is as true as the sun is in the heavens, that such language was made use of, and it was a common thing for all the pilgrims to curse the Indians, according to the order of their priests. It is also wonderful how they prayed, that they should pray the bullet through the Indian's heart, and their souls down into hell. If I had any faith in such prayers, I should begin to think that soon we should all be gone. However, if this is the way they pray, that is bullets through people's hearts, I hope they will not pray for me; I should rather be excused. But to say the least, there is no excuse for their ignorance how to treat their enemies, and pray for them. If the Dr. and his people had only turned to the 23d of Luke, and 34th verse, and heard the words of their Master, whom they pretended to follow, they would see that their course did utterly condemn them; or the 7th of Acts, and 60th verse, and heard the language of the pious Stephen, we think it vastly different from the pilgrims; he prayed, Lord, lay not this sin to their charge. No curses were heard from these pious martyrs.

I do not hesitate to say, that through the prayers, preaching, and examples of those pretended pious, has been the foundation of all the slavery and degradation in the American Colonies, towards colored people. Experience has taught me that this has been a most sorry and wretched doctrine to us poor ignorant Indians. I will mention two or three things to amuse you a little; that is, as I was passing through Connecticut, about 15 years ago, where they are so pious that they kill the cats for killing rats, and whip the beer barrels for working upon the Sabbath, that in a severe cold night, when the face of the earth was one glare of ice, dark and stormy, I called at a man's house to know if I could not stay with him, it being about nine miles to the house where I then lived, and knowing him to be a rich man, and with all very pious, knowing if he had a mind he could do it comfortably, and with all we were both members of one church. My reception, however, was almost as cold as the weather, only he did not turn me out of doors; if he had I knew not but I should have frozen to death. My situation was a little better than being out, for he allowed a little wood, but no bed, because

I was an Indian. Another Christian asked me to dine with him, and put my dinner behind the door; I thought this a queer compliment indeed.

About two years ago, I called at an inn in Lexington; and a gentleman present, not spying me to be an Indian, began to say they ought to be exterminated. I took it up in our defence, though not boisterous, but coolly; and when we came to retire, finding that I was an Indian, he was unwilling to sleep opposite my room, for fear of being murdered before morning. We presume his conscience plead guilty. These things I mention to show that the doctrines of the pilgrims has grown up with the people.

But not to forget Philip and his lady, and his prophecy: it is, (that is 1671,) when Philip went to Boston, his clothing was worth nearly one hundred dollars. It is said by some of the writers in those days, that their money being so curiously wrought, that neither Jew nor devil could counterfeit it. A high encomium upon Indian arts; and with it they used to adorn their Sagamores, in a curious manner. It was said that Philip's wife was neatly attired in the Indian style; some of the white females used to call her a proud woman, because she would not bow down to them, and was so particular in adorning herself. Perhaps while these ladies were so careful to review the Queen, they had forgot that she was truly one of the greatest women there was among them, although not quite so white. But While we censure others for their faults, in spending so much time to view their fair and handsome features, whether colored or white, we would remind all the fair sex it is what they all love, that is jewels and feathers. It was what the Indian women used to love, and still love. And customs, we presume, that the whites brought from their original savage fathers, 1000 years ago. Every white that knows their own history, knows there was not a whit difference between them and the Indians of their days.

But who was Philip, that made all this display in the world; that put an enlightened nation to flight, and won so many battles? It was a son of nature; with nature's talent alone. And who did he have to contend with? With all the combined arts of cultivated talents of the old and new world. It was like putting one talent against a thousand. And yet Philip with that, accomplished more than all of them. Yea, he out-did the well-disciplined forces of Greece, under the command of Philip, the Grecian Emperor; for he never was enabled to lay such plans of allying the tribes of the earth together, as Philip of Mount Hope did. And even Napoleon patterned after him, in collecting his forces and surprising the enemy. Washington, too, pursued many of his plans in attacking the enemy, and thereby enabled him to defeat his antagonists and conquer them. What, then, shall we say; shall we not do right to say that Philip, with his one talent, out-strips them all with their ten thousand? No warrior of any age, was ever known to pursue such plans as Philip did. And it is well known that Church and nobody else could have conquered, if his people had not used treachery, which was owing to their ignorance; and after all, it is a fact, that it was not the pilgrims that conquered him, it was Indians. And as to his benevolence, it was very great; no one in history can accuse Philip of being cruel to his conquered foes; that he used them with more hospitality than they, the pilgrims did, cannot be denied; and that he had knowledge and forethought, cannot be denied. As Mr. Gooking, in speaking of Philip says, that he was a man of good understanding and knowledge in the best things. Mr. Gooking it appears was a benevolent man, and a friend to Indians.

How deep then was the thought of Philip, when he could look from Maine to Georgia, and from the ocean to the lakes, and view with one look all his brethren withering before the more enlightened to come; and how true his prophesy, that the white people would not only cut down their groves, but would enslave them. Had the inspiration of Isaiah been there, he could not have been more correct. Our groves and hunting grounds are gone, our dead are dug up, our council-fires are put out, and a foundation was laid in the first Legislature, to enslave our people, by taking from them all rights which has been strictly adhered to ever since. Look at the disgraceful laws, disfranchising us as citizens. Look at the treaties made by Congress, all broken. Look at the deep-rooted plans laid, when a territory becomes a State, that after so many years, the laws shall be extended over the Indians that live within their boundaries. Yea, every charter that has been given, was given with the view of driving the Indians out of the States, or dooming them to become chained under desperate laws, that would make them drag out a miserable life as one chained to the galley; and this is the course that has been pursued for nearly two hundred years. A fire, a canker, created by the pilgrims from across the Atlantic, to burn and destroy my poor unfortunate brethren, and it cannot be denied. What then shall we do, shall we cease crying, and say it is all wrong, or shall we bury the hatchet and those unjust laws, and Plymouth Rock together, and become friends. And will the sons of the pilgrims aid in putting out the fire and destroying the canker that will ruin all that their fathers left behind them to destroy? (by this we see how true Philip spake.) If so, we hope we shall not hear it said from ministers and church members, that we are so good no other people can live with us, as you know it is a common thing for them to say, Indians cannot live among Christian people; no, even the President of the United States tells the Indians they cannot live among civilized people, and we want your lands, and must have them, and will have them. As if he had said to them, we want your lands for our use to speculate upon, it aids us in paying off our national debt and supporting us in Congress, to drive you off.

You see, my red children, that our fathers carried on this scheme of getting your lands for our use, and we have now become rich and powerful; and we have a right to do with you just as we please; we claim to be your fathers. And we think we shall do you a great favor, my dear sons and daughters, to drive you out, to get you away out of the reach of our civilized people, who are cheating you, for we have no law to reach them, we cannot protect you although you be our children. So it is no use, you need not cry, you must go, even if the lions devour you, for we promised the land you have to somebody else long ago, perhaps twenty or thirty years; and we did it without your consent, it is true. But this has been the way our fathers first brought us up, and it is hard to depart from it; therefore you shall have no protection from us. Now while we sum up this subject. Does it not appear that the cause of all wars from beginning to end, was and is for the want of good usage? That the whites have always been the aggressors, and the wars, cruelties and blood shed is a job of their own seeking, and not the Indians? Did you ever know of Indians' hurting those who was kind to them? No. We have a thousand witnesses to the contrary. Yea, every male and female declare it to be the fact. We often hear of the wars breaking out upon the frontiers, and it is because the same spirit reigns there that reigned here in New England; and wherever there are any Indians, that spirit still reigns; and at present, there is no law to stop it. What, then, is to be done; let every friend of the Indians now seize the mantle of Liberty and throw it over those burning elements that has spread with such fearful rapidity, and at once extinguish them forever. It is true, that now and then a feeble voice has been raised in our favor. Yes, we might speak of distinguished men, but they fall so far short in the minority, that it is heard but at a small distance. We want trumpets that sound like thunder, and men to act as though they were going at war with those corrupt and degrading principles that robs one of all rights, merely because he is ignorant, and of a little different color. Let us have principles that will give every one his due; and then shall wars cease, and the weary find rest. Give the Indian his rights, and you may be assured war will cease.

But, by this time you have been enabled to see that Philip's prophesy has come to pass; therefore, as a man of natural abilities, I shall pronounce him the greatest man that was ever in America; and so it will stand, until he is proved to the contrary, to the everlasting disgrace of the pilgrims' fathers.

We will now give you his language in the Lord's Prayer.

Noo-chun kes-uk-qut-tiam-at-am unch koo-we-su-onk, kuk-ket-as-soo-tam-oonk pey-au-moo-utch, keet-te-nan-tam-oo-onk ne nai; ne-ya-ne ke-suk-qutkah oh-ke-it; aos-sa-ma-i-in-ne-an ko-ko-ke-suk-o-da-e nut-as-e-suk-ok-ke fu-tuk-qun-neg; kah ah-quo-an-tam-a-i-in-ne-an num-match-e-se-ong-an-on-ash, ne-match-ene-na-mun wonk neet-ah-quo-antam-au-o-un-non-og nish-noh pasuk noo-na-mortuk-quoh-who-nan, kah chaque sag-kom-pa-ginne-an en qutch-e-het-tu-ong-a-nit, qut poh-qud-wus-sin-ne-an watch match-i-tut.

Having now given historical facts, and an exposition in relation to ancient times, by which we have been enabled to discover the foundation which destroyed our common fathers, in their struggle together; it was indeed nothing more than the spirit of avarice and usurpation of power, that has brought people in all ages to hate and devour each other. And I cannot for one moment look back upon what is past, and call it religion. No, it has not the least appearance like it. Do not then wonder, my dear friends, at my bold and unpolished statements; though I do not believe that truth wants any polishing whatever. And I can assure you, that I have no design to tell an untruth, but facts alone. Oft have I been surprised at the conduct of those who pretend to be Christians, to see how they were affected towards those who were of a different cast, professing one faith. Yes, the spirit of degradation has always been exercised towards us poor and untaught people. If we cannot read, we can see and feel; and we find no excuse in the Bible for Christians conducting towards us as they do.

It is said that in the Christian's guide, that God is merciful, and they that are his followers are like him. How much mercy do you think has been shown towards Indians, their wives and their children? Not much, we think. No. And ye fathers, I will appeal to you that are white. Have you any regard for your wives and children, for those delicate sons and daughters? Would you like to see them slain and laid in heaps, and their bodies devoured by the vultures and wild beasts of prey? and their bones bleaching in the sun and air, till they moulder away, or were covered by the falling leaves of the forest, and not resist? No. Your hearts would break with grief, and with all the religion and knowledge you have, it would not impede your force to take vengeance upon your foe, that had so cruelly conducted thus, although God has forbid you in so doing. For he has said, vengeance is mine, and I will repay. What, then, my dear affectionate friends, can you think of those who have been so often betrayed, routed and stripped of all they possess, of all their kindred in the flesh? Can, or do you think we have no feeling? The speech of Logan, the white man's friend, is no doubt fresh in your memory, that he intended to live and die the friend of the white man; that he always fed them and gave them the best his cabin afforded; and he appealed to them if they had not been well used; to which they never denied. After which, they murdered all of his family in cool blood; which roused his passions to be revenged upon the whites. This circumstance is but one in a thousand.

Upon the banks of Ohio, a party of two hundred white warriors, in 1757, or about that time, came across a settlement of Christian Indians, and falsely accused them of being warriors; to which they denied, but all to no purpose; they were determined to massacre them all. They, the Indians, then asked liberty to prepare for the fatal hour, The white savages then gave them one hour, as the historian said. They then prayed together; and in tears and cries, upon their knees, begged pardon of each other, of all they had done. After which, they informed the white savages that they were now ready. One white man then begun with a mallet, and knocked them down, and continued his work until he had killed fifteen, with his own hand; then saying it ached, he gave his commission to another. And thus they continued till they had massacred nearly ninety men, women and children, all these innocent of any crime. What sad tales are these for us to look upon the massacre of our dear fathers, mothers, brothers and sisters; and if we speak, we are then called savages for complaining. Our affections for each other, are the same as yours; we think as much of ourselves as you do of yourselves. When our children are sick, we do all we can for them; they lie buried deep in our affections; if they die, we remember it long, and mourn in after years. Children also cleave to their parents; they look to them for aid, they do the best they know how to do for each other; and when strangers come among us, we use them as well as we know how; we feel honest in whatever we do, we have no desire to offend any one. But when we are so deceived, it spoils all our confidence in our visitors. And although I can say that I have some dear, good friends among white people, yet I eye them with a jealous eye, for fear they will betray me. Having been deceived so much by them, how can I help it; being brought up to look upon white people as being enemies and not friends, and by the whites treated as such, who can wonder? Yes, in vain have I looked for the Christian to take me by the hand and bid me welcome to his cabin, as my fathers did them, before we were born; and if they did, it was only to satisfy curiosity, and not to look upon me as a man and a Christian. And so all of my people have been treated, whether Christians or not. I say then, a different course must be pursued, and different laws must be enacted, and all men must operate under one general law. And while you ask yourselves, what do they, the Indians, want? you have only to look at the unjust laws made for them, and say they want what I want, in order to make men of them, good and wholesome citizens. And this plan ought to be pursued by all missionaries, or not pursued at all. That is not only to make Christians of us, but men; which plan as yet has never been pursued. And when it is, I will then throw my might upon the side of missions, and do what I can to favor it. But this work must begin here first, in New England.

Having now closed, I would say that many thanks is due from me to you, though an unworthy speaker, for your kind attention; and I wish you to understand that we are thankful for every favor; and you and I have to rejoice that we have not to answer for our fathers' crimes, neither shall we do right to charge them one to another. We can only regret it, and flee from it, and from henceforth, let peace and righteousness be written upon our hearts and hands forever, is the wish of a poor Indian.

A Note About the Author

William Apes (1798–1839) was a Pequot writer, activist, and minister. Born in northwestern Massachusetts, he was raised in a family of mixed Pequot, African, and European descent. On his mother's side, he claimed King Philip—a Wampanoag sachem who was assassinated by Plymouth colonists—as his ancestor. Following their parents' separation, William and his siblings were taken to their maternal grandparents, who abused and neglected them. Soon, they were taken in by local families as indentured servants. At fifteen, he ran away to join a New York militia, serving in the War of 1812, where he developed a lifelong addiction to alcohol. In 1821, having returned to his Pequot family in Massachusetts, Apes married Mary Wood, with whom he had four children. He was ordained a Protestant Methodist minister in 1829, and in the same year published his groundbreaking autobiography *A Son of the Forest*. Written as a response to the United States government's policy of Indian Removal, *A Son of the Forest* was one of the first of its kind from a Native American author, earning Apes a reputation as a leading advocate for his people. In the last decade of his life, Apes worked tirelessly as an activist, lecturer, and writer, supporting the 1833 Mashpee Revolt on Cape Cod and delivering a powerful eulogy on King Philip in 1836.

A Note from the Publisher

Spanning many genres, from non-fiction essays to literature classics to children's books and lyric poetry, Mint Edition books showcase the master works of our time in a modern new package. The text is freshly typeset, is clean and easy to read, and features a new note about the author in each volume. Many books also include exclusive new introductory material. Every book boasts a striking new cover, which makes it as appropriate for collecting as it is for gift giving. Mint Edition books are only printed when a reader orders them, so natural resources are not wasted. We're proud that our books are never manufactured in excess and exist only in the exact quantity they need to be read and enjoyed.

bookfinity™

Discover more of your favorite classics with Bookfinity™.

- Track your reading with custom book lists.
- Get great book recommendations for your personalized Reader Type.
- Add reviews for your favorite books.
- AND MUCH MORE!

Visit **bookfinity.com** and take the fun Reader Type quiz to get started.

Enjoy our classic and modern companion pairings!

Classic & Modern

www.ingramcontent.com/pod-product-compliance
Lightning Source LLC
Chambersburg PA
CBHW020443030426
42337CB00014B/1369